~~~ **A Fa**

SURVIVING TRAUMATIC LOSS

OVERCOMING TRAGEDY

By Molly Hanna Glidden

~~~~~~

Illustrated by Brooke M. Delmonaco

ISBN-13:978-1975952020

Self-Published

Disclaimer: The author has tried to recreate events,
locales and conversations from Marie Herndon's
memories of them. In order to maintain all
anonymity, the names of individuals
have been changed.

Dedication

*This book is dedicated to the mothers and fathers who have lost a child,
for it is a tragedy when a parent outlives their son or daughter.*
~~~
To the families who have lost a family member killed in the line of duty.

~~~

A Special Thanks to our Massachusetts State Police for keeping us safe.

~~~

~May peace and healing be found in our less-than-perfect world. ~

Table of Contents

A Family Broken – Surviving Traumatic Loss

Chapter 1

The Baby Boomer Years

For the most part, family life during the '50s and '60s was a simpler time, just like the old black and white televisions with few stations at no cost. Moms were busy tending to children and chores, while breadwinning, rule-making dads took care of finances. Most families had a single-income household, and marriage vows were taken seriously, for better or for worse. A lot of this was due to strong religious morals and the long-held belief that one's reputation in town was of great importance. This meant keeping a family together no matter what obstacles were encountered. What was never up for negotiation was the devotion parents had for one another as well as for their family.

Middle class families had strived for the perfect family life back then. Many TV shows contributed to people's notion of what real marriages and family life should be. A few memorable shows were; *Leave It to Beaver,* *The Donna Reed Show,* and *Ozzie and Harriet.* All claimed to represent real families, however it wasn't long before people realized these shows were for entertainment. Millions of Americans didn't have the perfect lifestyle depicted on the small screens back then. On a positive note, the actors and actresses did represent positive role models, a big difference from many of today's shows.

How was life different from those half-hour shows of the past? For one thing, responsibility for raising children fell heavily on the mother. Looking back, we can now see attending to children and being a homemaker was much harder than what TV shows portrayed. Although fathers were absent most of the day, they played an important role. More often than not, the man of the house was responsible for being the strict disciplinarian: "spare the rod, spoil the child." This was the viewpoint of most parents during this time period. Even corporal punishment was acceptable back then. Family members along with the outside world respected the head of household. There was never interference with the way children were raised. When punishment was deemed necessary, the child took the punishment with a stiff upper lip and with little or no recourse. There were rules to obey and chores to be done. Although harsh punishment was available, it was rarely needed in keeping children in line. Of course many of us remember how it hung over us like lightning that could strike at any time!

Religion during this era played a much bigger role in family life. Many families attended church together and parents often sent their children of the Catholic faith to private Catholic schools. Parochial schools were the norm, with one or more such schools in almost every town. Parents wanted the best education and protection available to their children. Of course, Catholic schools were not for everyone. Academically, many children excelled in parochial schools more than those attending public schools. If a child could not keep up with the other 40 or more children in class, there was little recourse. Children either did their best to meet the high standards or suffered the embarrassment of being kept back another year. Back then, if a child had challenges not easily recognized, he or she was left to deal with their own shortcomings. There were no special needs classes for children with disorders such as ADHD or dyslexia. Most family doctors didn't recognize these medical conditions, therefore there was little help for a struggling child. This lack of knowledge created intolerance on the teacher's part for students with these disorders. Children who could not sit still were considered fidgety and if they couldn't focus or keep up in class, they were thought of as being slow. Their peers often picked on these children, calling them class clowns, troublemakers, or just plain antisocial. Even more serious were those children who rebelled, acting out in more drastic ways. Most importantly, how difficult it must have been for them. Back then there were no medications or counseling for these now treatable disorders. These children were often shuffled off to public schools, sometimes in the middle of the year.

Looking back, as a young Catholic girl who attended parochial schools, there was much emphasis placed on religion and education, followed closely by behavior. It was commonplace for many children to receive discipline at the hands of the nuns. Of course the religious teachers who taught Catholic school were allowed and encouraged to take disciplinary action whenever they felt it was necessary. Too often, the punishment did not fit the behavior and it was generally harsh. To the adults, the child was rarely if ever right in most any given situation. Many parents were not interested in how the accused child might have felt—after all, these teachers were people of God who took vows and wore the habit. Their words were gospel. In spite of it all, most parochial school children grew into healthy adults remaining as Christians today.

The decline of parishioners over the years has been due to many Catholics seeking God through solitude. It seemed, for many, there was less of a need for a structured religion or for attendance at mass. This trend began during the tumultuous social revolution of the '60s. Regardless of changing times, most of the church's basic teachings still remain within the hearts and souls of many in spite of the antiquated laws still remaining today.

Large families were the norm in those days. Being one of six children, I know there were many challenges, and we survived. It wasn't unusual to see families with eight or more children. There was a lovely family with 15 children living in our neighborhood.

Very little emphasis was put on money or material things back then. Remember when water was free? There was no bottled water! Families made it work, learning to live with or without. Middle class families were grateful to have furniture passed down from past generations. There was always a secondhand furniture store to be found. It was fun browsing for odd pieces from a different time. Families today rarely settle on anything less than new. Of course, today, the cost of living is way out of control. With both parents or couples working and the lack of time, this could be a factor in why there are fewer children. Maintaining big houses and raising children has become unbelievably expensive.

Just a few generations ago, children were taught to be seen and not heard around adults. Any conversation with our parents was mostly done at the dinner table. Of course Mom thought best that we share only good news so that dad could unwind after a long hard day.

As children, we were compliant because the alternative was never pleasant. Just the same, we were no worse off and knew our place in the world.

Remembering back to our dinner meals, the liver and onions or the corned beef and cabbage our mother would place in front of us were the toughest meals to swallow! Instinctively we knew 'no' wasn't an option as there would be no dessert or nothing more to eat and those hunger pains would last all night! Of course we were always overjoyed to see our dog Brandy napping under the table—trouble was he always left evidence of peas and onions for Mom to pick up. Being the peacemaker, she cleaned up without reporting to Dad. Mom was not only the best secret keeper; she was also the best mom and chef. Of course, like most kids, the realization of all good things parents do is never realized until we are grown and on our own.

During this time period, it was nothing to see most children hiking to school in the freezing cold and deep snow. For some of us it was more than a mile. We were safe walking alone back then. However, due to the fact that most families had only one car, we didn't expect rides from our parents. Children today somehow cannot grasp those days. In their defense, however, safety has become a major issue in today's unsafe world.

As my memory continues to unfold, thoughts drift back to coming home from school, opening the back door, and smelling the wonderful aroma of hot apple pies cooling. On Fridays, Mom would bake her special oatmeal cookies with chocolate chips! Oftentimes Mom would forge ahead regardless of how bad she might have felt. There were days when her hands and knuckles would be so swollen and painful due to arthritis. I can still remember the unpleasant smell of the Ben-Gay she so often used. The deep love she carried in her heart for all her children kept her going. Mom's top priority was to make sure her family stayed together in peace and harmony—never an easy task.

As I've grown older, I'm able to look back at my own experiences. I feel privileged to have been a part of childrearing. It's obvious to all there has been a great deal of change in how children are being raised today. In most households, there are two working parents, thus allowing fathers to have more hands on when it comes to their kids. This makes for more quality time creating stability and better self-esteem within each child—another positive change we have seen over the past few generations.

What had started in the '60s with the 'me generation of boomers' is now called the 'me, me millennial generation'. A real sense of entitlement has developed and the 'selfies' seem to be all over social media. Building self-esteem with over the top adoration and little discipline can leave some kids with narcissistic tendencies.

It's also becoming apparent that there are fewer basic manners being taught, like *ladies before gentlemen,* and fewer doors being held open for another. Remember when crossing the street meant waiting for all cars to go by or running to avoid vehicles? Today it's become a walker's entitlement! What happened to 'respecting others' as was taught back then? Young children from the '50s and '60s had certain values such as common courtesy, especially for their elders. Much of that has been lost over time. Whomever we addressed growing up, it was respectfully Mr. or Mrs., Aunt or Uncle.

More and more families are dining in restaurants with many showing little common courtesy. Parents of my generation inevitably knew a two-year-old could not be reasoned with! The mother often took control of the situation, taking an unruly child outside due to respect for other diners. It was a rarity to hear raised voices in a restaurant back then. Now it's much more common to see an out-of-control child having a loud discussion with a parent. This lack of consideration is often noticed throughout restaurants.

As a baby boomer looking back, there is a sense that we were no worse off growing up during those turbulent years. Whether parents' decisions were right or wrong, they did their best and lessons were learned. As parents of children who have grown, one can look back and see the good things, the mistakes, and imperfections. I can also say that in some ways, our parents had it better. Mom stayed home cooking wonderful meals, doing all the household chores along with caring for her children. The Moms of today have more pressures forcing them to multitask as most work outside the home.

It's certainly a different way of life from yesteryear. My sense is that the pendulum needs to start swinging back in the other direction, allowing for a kinder, gentler, and more caring generation to once again evolve.

As I continue my reflection on childhood, playing outside till dinnertime was something all children looked forward to. Whether it was pouring rain or blinding snow, we stayed out for hours finding good and creative ways of having fun. Being outdoors was healthy and Mom could concentrate on household duties while we were exploring and finding our independence. During winter months we would build snowmen and igloos as a reward for helping Dad shovel the driveway. In summer, we would get creative, such as finding leftover materials to build our own huts or tree houses. We made signs out of wood or cardboard that read: 'Keep Out.' Children back then were allowed to work out their own ideas and problems. Parents often encouraged this.

Every fall after the autumn leaves had tumbled down, families would be seen outdoors cleaning yards and raking together. There were no sounds of leaf blowers, just the sounds of laughter as children jumped into leaves piled high. One of my fondest childhood memories was the smell of burning leaves on weekends. Of course, leaf burning is no longer allowed due to changing times. Since the '70s, communities across the country implemented laws forbidding this tradition due to air pollution and its health risks. My dad saw the ripe old age of 93 regardless of the many years he had burned piles of leaves! Just the same, fall was always the time to prepare for the cold New England winter. The firemen in our town would begin burning down the bogs, allowing outdoor skating for all! We never minded the lumpy ice we skated on, we'd fallen many times only to get up feeling proud that we finally learned how to skate on our own. Our feet would be tired and frozen but we walked home regardless. Once home and in our bedroom, each toe one by one would slowly begin to thaw under the covers. At times the pain was unbearable, however the love for skating made it all worthwhile!

When spring and summer would finally arrive, neighborhood kids could be seen playing baseball, basketball, kickball, hopscotch, or tag. Many would be riding bikes and yes, without helmets! Boys would be making their own jumping ramps on the street, living dangerously. It wasn't uncommon to see the neighborhood daredevils—boys carrying pocket knives or playing with a BB gun. Often times you would see girls playing with the boys and they were called 'tomboys!' We rode in cars with no seat belts and it wasn't uncommon to see kids hanging out the windows. Riding in our dad's new station wagon was fun until I decided to ride in the third seat that faced backwards. Carsickness happened almost every time! And for many kids, going in the house for a snack meant passing through clouds of blue cigarette smoke...yet we somehow survived!

The sky was the limit and those summer days were ours. There were playground activities during summer and it was free! And yes, if someone got hurt, lawsuits were unheard of. It was called an accident and there were few. Older teens often volunteered to be playground leaders. They watched over the younger children, making it a full day of fun. Some of the games we played and friends we made left the best of memories.

Unfortunately many of the games today are geared toward electronics being played at home alone. The downside for some children is that they spend too much time only to become addicted to these games. Outdoor sports, such as school team sports, are healthier options but can be too competitive and structured. This leaves questions as to how children learn to enjoy alone times as well as mingle freely amongst friends. We do find ourselves living in constantly changing times and yet we seem to adapt. In some ways, these changes and new innovations certainly make life easier for all!

Going back in time, neighbors were your friends. Families would look out for one another and help when they could. Today there seems to be less neighborhood bonding and for those who are elderly living alone, this can create feelings of isolation. My thinking in this regard is that people are so busy they are simply overextended. Family life is hectic, and time is of the essence, because so many parents are in the workplace.

I can remember back when that one dollar bill could always be stretched and made to last! A family could live in a large home with one working parent. For a man, a respectable job meant delivering mail, working at a manufacturing plant, or being a salesman. This was not only a reasonable living, it supported a big family. I remember milk trucks, laundry trucks, and the sound of ice cream trucks driving through the neighborhood—wow, what wonderful memories indeed! Certainly those days seemed to have brought far less stress. Of course some of this was because the population in the suburbs was small by today's comparison. There was less traffic, cheap gas around 25 cents a gallon, and food prices were reasonable. Small towns meant low property taxes!

There was a downside to the turbulent '60s however. The most memorable was the assassination of our great president John F. Kennedy in 1963 and of his brother, the late Robert F. Kennedy, in 1968. Most everyone who lived in the '60s remembered exactly where they were when the dreadful news of our late president's death was released. These truly great losses not only affected the Kennedy family but touched the hearts of all Americans. The other most memorable was the Viet Nam War which had taken so many of our brave soldiers. This war divided our great nation politically.

The '60s also began a time of major social change. Those who lived through this period will remember the traumatic events of those historic years. The result of this era marked the beginning of the 'me' generation. It began the fight for freedom and rights. Young adults striking out for independence became the norm. There were many who did not do well with this kind of freedom, especially the young adults who left home far too early and were unprepared for life ahead. The '60s brought tie-dyed shirts, sit-ins, and hippies smoking marijuana. Drugs back then didn't seem to cause many deaths. Today there is an epidemic of drug overdoses with deaths of up to 100 Americans every day.

Among the tragedies of the baby boomer era was the large cohort of young adults forced into war right out of high school. There were tens of thousands of casualties, terrible war crimes committed, and way too many lives lost and broken. Now, half a century later, you will find many Viet Nam vets continuing to struggle with battle scars. This war had a terrible impact on America and their families.

For the young adults who were not drafted, drugs and sexual freedom had become more prevalent. Many who didn't go to college married young. It was not the norm for women to go off to college in the early '60s. Those who stayed home after high school had few choices, leaving many young women ill prepared for life ahead. For many, marriage became commonplace after high school or college. During this era, the average age for women entering marriage was 19 to 22.

It was extremely difficult when a young pregnant teen had a child. The only options had been to keep the child or give the baby up for adoption. Although birth control pills were introduced in the early 1960s, parents rarely discussed anything to do with sex. After all, the Pill might have perpetuated promiscuity.

Becoming a teen mom or dad certainly forced one to grow up rather quickly, especially when a marriage took place. There were no tools or instruction manuals, therefore many muddled through learning the hard way. Today's young adults have many choices and options eliminating 'yesterday's shotgun weddings,' one of the relics of another time. This alone has been a huge advantage for all young women today.

The average age for marriage today is 29 to 35 or older. Much is due to positive changes made in the last several decades. Many men and women go to college only to return home due to their financial status. Some remain home well into their late twenties and beyond. Again the high cost of living, paying off student debt and the lack of full time jobs seem to be the reason. Being home allows time for maturity and savings when parents are on board. Many young adults do seem comfortable living at home.

In years past, many young marriages ended in divorce. This proved to the next generation that delaying marriage would allow more time in finding a suitable partner. It also prepares couples to develop better parenting skills through maturity, patience, and hard work. Due to better education for both men and women, waiting longer to begin a family makes more sense in this fast-paced world. Today's marriages with or without children at an older age have allowed for better financial stability.

My greatest childhood memories always return me to holidays with family. There was Easter—getting dressed up for Mass in outfits our mom either sewed or purchased out of the Sears catalog. The joy of Easter morning included patiently waiting for the egg hunts with our brand new Easter bonnets and baskets. It seemed no matter who got the most eggs, in the end they had to be shared amongst siblings. Looking back, why didn't my siblings or I ever question the Easter bunny that never did appear? I'm certain that, if questions had been raised, the bunny might have disappeared only to be gone forever!

And oh, remembering those family Christmas parties when different Santas would come to our house every year. One clear memory was the year that Santa forgot his black boots. His shoes looked just like the ones our neighbor wore. Even his voice seemed far too familiar. No matter what, I stayed in that place of denial even after my older brother whispered in my ear that Santa was a fake! Seeing those shoes should have confirmed everything. One thing was certain, the denial thing definitely felt good! After all, once it was bedtime on Christmas Eve, the excitement of something awaiting us under the tree was a guaranteed yearly event! Looking back, there seemed to be lots of presents on Christmas morning but then again, there were six of us. Once all the gifts were ripped open in what seemed no time at all, there was less than expected and most were practical. There would always be shirts, sweaters, pajamas, and slippers. Despite this fact there was always the spirit of the holiday with the wonderful aroma of turkey and baked pies coming from Mom's kitchen.

Of course going from denial to acceptance that 'Santa' wasn't real seemed the hardest childhood fantasy to let go! It was the first of many disappointments in life with bigger ones just around the corner. Thankfully those Magic 8 balls and Ouija boards we played with had never come true—well, maybe once! Seeing one's future in advance just may be far too painful for some. In spite of the many disappointments and tragedies that lay ahead, painful events are what help to shape us throughout life. All our difficult experiences build character and strength, giving us the ability to feel compassion and empathy toward others. More importantly, no matter how many years pass by or what happens along the way, it's our strong family ties and traditions that hold us together offsetting the inevitable heartaches to come.

As with any family, when it comes to tragedy, no one is immune. No matter where you are or what you are doing, no one is exempt from bad things happening. We genuinely feel compassion for those going through tragic loss and most of us silently say to ourselves, "this could never happen to me." If we live long enough, there will be some type of stressful event in our lives. Keep in mind that, no matter how bad a situation is, life eventually presents us with a new day and a wonderful sunrise for us to embrace.

In the next chapter you'll find the story of a lovely couple in post-WWII America, raising a family during the '50s and '60s. This family suffered several tragic losses far greater than the normal family. A beautiful baby never having a chance to experience life, suicides, and a horrific murder! Most people find it unimaginable for any mother or father to lose a child. However when the Herndon family thought that life couldn't get any worse, it most certainly did!

A Family Broken - Surviving Traumatic Loss

Chapter 2

A Family Cursed?

The Herndons, a prominent middle class family, had been living in the western suburbs of Boston for generations. Many of the family's ancestors came to this once-small town from Ireland, England, and Canada. Approximately eight generations of Herndons have settled in the same area dating back to the 1800s.

What tragic events impacted this wonderful hard working family?

There is a parallel with the tragedies of the famous Kennedy family. It seemed they were living under a curse destining several members to early deaths. That being said, we all do experience death and loss the longer we live. Tragic loss is when we lose family members who never had a chance to either grow up or see their golden years.

The Story of Tragic Losses

Thomas and Elizabeth Herndon were the parents of seven beautiful children, three boys and four girls. They were living the American dream until one tragedy after another began to take its toll.

Mr. Herndon often compared the many losses in his later years to those of the Kennedys. Thomas and Elizabeth already experienced the natural end of life such as the loss of their elderly parents. Both, however, suffered the loss of siblings before their time: Elizabeth's tragic loss of her young brother, killed in war, and Thomas's brother due to depression and alcoholism.

Real devastation came when they had to bury three of their seven children as well as their granddaughter. These tragedies left the parents with broken hearts, and the negative impact also affected their remaining children.

Siblings in tragic circumstances often bury their deep pain only to find it surfacing in unsuspecting ways later in life. This kind of emotional pain is similar to the distress of those coming home from war suffering from PTSD.

Thomas and Elizabeth worked tirelessly, raising a big family during the baby boomer era and beyond. Their love and guidance were top priority. Like most parents, life's greatest reward was watching their children grow into happy and healthy adults.

They never imagined burying one child, let alone surviving three plus a grandchild!

As any parent knows, when it comes to child rearing, questions arise. One in particular; 'How do parents give each child the right tools to withstand life's blows?' Why does one sibling grow strong emotionally while another can't seem to attain coping skills to get through life's difficulties? Could it be the ingrained personality and character that allows these blows to sway one child while knocking down another? In big families, it's usually older siblings who have the highest of expectations from parents. Generally speaking they tend to become most independent. Oftentimes, middle children don't seem to feel these expectations from their parents. Many can get lost in the shuffle, having a harder time finding inner resources to rely on. This also can happen with the youngest of a large family. The last child tends to be seen as the 'forever baby,' making it hard for parents to let go if at all.

The youngest of the Herndons seemed to take the most time in finding his purpose in life. Many of his major decisions included a lot of procrastination. A big assumption would be that, in part, he didn't want to make some of the mistakes of his older siblings. Another possibility could be that getting close to his siblings could bring pain if there were to be another loss. This may explain his remaining at home until his early thirties and waiting until his mid-forties to marry and have children. Just the same, the Herndon children all had unique and wonderful qualities regardless of circumstances.

During their first decade of marriage, Thomas and Elizabeth lost hope of having children. They tried for several years, only to lose their firstborn son during childbirth. It wasn't long after when a beautiful baby girl named Barbara came into their life with hopes of adoption. However, before the process of adoption was over, the birth mother reached out in desperation to have her daughter back. No matter how much Elizabeth came to love Barbara, she understood. At the same time, Elizabeth discovered she had finally become pregnant. With time and prayer, sorrows faded as both began counting their blessings.

Thomas Jr., first-born and the oldest son of the Herndons, was a real welcome into the world! A perfectly handsome nine-pound baby boy born in 1946. His first three years got him plenty of loving attention, but that was before his curly-haired sister Marie arrived in 1949.

Those were good years. Thomas Sr. was a police officer, and during his spare time he helped with chores on his dad's farm. The farm is where the Herndons lived early on in marriage. The trees needed spraying and the apples needed picking, making for much work to be done. With two children and another on the way, the family outgrew their small cottage on the farm in 1950. Together they found a lovely Cape-style home across town in a kid-friendly neighborhood. No sooner had they moved in, when Thomas Jr. and Marie discovered they had a new baby sister named Melinda, born in 1951. She was just as sweet as the other two but now, Thomas Jr. was outnumbered. In 1952 an adorable sister named Sara was born. This was tough on a little fella, as all the attention he was used to had now gone to his three sisters!

Some years had passed when 9-year-old Thomas Jr. was told he now had a new baby brother. However, it wasn't long before he realized this newborn was way too small to play ball. The new bundle of joy named Matthew was born in 1956. Another handsome baby boy with big cheeks and curls just like his oldest sister. Thomas Jr. continued to be independent, playing outside the home with his newfound friends. His parents found themselves very busy as the family continued to grow. Just one year later came the biggest surprise of all! James and Joan were born in 1957. They were the cutest set of twins all wrapped in pink and blue! It was a busy and exciting time for everyone.

As far as having any more children, Elizabeth would finally lay down the law with Thomas: "No more storks dropping bundles of joy by the Herndon residence!" Elizabeth's great love for her children filled her heart but her hands were full. Thomas Sr. was not a 'hands on' kind of a guy at home. For him, working and making money was the priority, which was very common in those days.

Besides being a full-time police officer, Thomas Sr. started another career part-time. He became a great and successful salesman. His self-employment eventually turned into his full-time job after retiring from the Police Department. Thomas Sr. maintained a small office in the living room of his second home; however, this had to change. The three babies, all in diapers, were just down the hall, well within earshot of his office. The older children couldn't watch the only TV in the living room except on Sunday nights. Before long, Thomas and Elizabeth found a much larger house closer to town. They chose a beautiful home everyone loved. Most importantly, it had separate office space. In time, this was where the Herndons made their happiest of memories and remained until their children left home.

First Tragic Loss for the Herndons

Joan, the sweetest baby girl, had just turned 8 months. Elizabeth would put her in the prettiest dresses often placing her in a small basket where little Joan felt comfortable and secure. She was so content propped up on the couch with family. Her pretty little eyes were often fixated on her twin brother James who was already crawling and having fun with his other siblings. Joan was the quietest and least demanding baby of all. She was the smaller of the twins, both being midlife babies. Joan had been born with Down syndrome along with a hole in her heart. Elizabeth knew that every day having her was a blessing from God. She also knew that one day any infection could kill her. Back in the 1950s, the technology to successfully fix her little heart was not available as it is today. The family adored Joan, oftentimes seeing her as their little angel.

One day an eerie dark cloud quietly settled over the Herndon home. Baby Joan had developed pneumonia. Later that evening she spiked a fever as she lay dying in her mother's arms. All the love and nurturing could not save her. It was so painfully difficult for Elizabeth who loved and cared for her baby girl.

The death of baby Joan was the first loss experienced by the Herndons' children. For them to have their sibling, their beautiful baby sister taken away, was tragic and incomprehensible. The black cloud continued to linger over the house for some time. It was this kind of loss that began the subtle changes within each and every family member. In order to cope, this family came to believe Joan had truly become their little angel. The family being Catholic, had Joan buried in a small white casket believing she was being delivered back to heaven. Baby Joan was deeply loved by all. Sadly, the deep sense of loss due to final separation never truly left her twin James.

The move to their new home certainly helped to bring some joy back to the family. As time marched on, the children were thriving, finding lots of friends in their new neighborhood. There were the usual issues as with all families but life was good for the most part. The youngest son James finally started school while the oldest son Thomas had graduated from Catholic High. As with many young men during the Viet Nam era, being drafted wasn't an option for Thomas Jr. It was determined at that time he would join the Navy. Elizabeth worried about her oldest son going off as most moms did. Time flew by and, after two years of being in the service, Thomas Jr. came home on leave to find the woman he fell in love with waiting for him. After a year or so, Thomas and his girlfriend Megan married. While still in the Navy, they lived in Virginia to finish out his career. During that time their first child was born before they returned home. With another child soon to arrive, Thomas Jr. decided to go back to school for his Master's degree in law enforcement. In some ways, Thomas had begun to follow in his father's footsteps.

It was 1968 when Marie, the Herndons' oldest daughter, was preparing to graduate from high school. She loved sports, having played on girls' basketball and tennis teams. Marie knew early on that if she wanted new clothes or those 45 record hits, she needed to make money. She babysat for several families until she got her worker's permit at 14½. Her first job was in a local supermarket within walking distance so she could work after school and on Saturdays. Her first love was tennis, practicing any chance she could. Playing first singles in high school gave her much joy due to her competitive spirit. In her last year of school, she, along with her friends, decided to enter a beauty contest in town. Coming in first runner-up brought much pride to her family. It was during this time period when Marie discovered she was pregnant. This upset Marie and her parents. However, even though she was of age, any decision-making was out of her hands at the time. Marie's father set things in motion for adoption. Rules were strict in many homes and problem solving was often done by the head of household. Reluctantly, Marie flew out to Virginia to live with her brother Thomas

Jr. and his new wife Megan until her baby was born. Within weeks, it became difficult for Marie. She was having constant anxiety and feeling homesick. Although Marie felt welcome, the young couple's apartment was small and she wasn't happy interfering in her brother's new life. Meanwhile, back home, Marie's boyfriend Larry found a way to get in touch with her. He expressed his love and asked if she would come home and marry him. With heartfelt thought and prayer, Marie concluded that even though she was only 19, giving her baby up was not an option. She had come to the realization that she already loved her child and the baby's father. She returned home to marry and together they would become a family. It was a difficult time with little to no support the first few years. Larry's mother had been kind, helping them get started in a small apartment, even though she had little money herself. Everything the newlyweds owned was secondhand, and they learned by doing things the hard way. The two teenagers had little knowledge of the new adult responsibilities that lay ahead. Nevertheless, months passed by and their beautiful baby girl was born. Soon better things were on the horizon. Marie's father realized it was time to accept and enjoy his new granddaughter Lisa. Elizabeth's prayers were answered.

It wasn't long after Marie and her husband had settled down when her middle sister Melinda found herself pregnant facing similar circumstance. It wasn't uncommon in the early to mid-'60s for women in their late teen years to find themselves with a steady boyfriend. It was a time period where there were few to no birth control options. It was more difficult for Melinda because, even though she was treated as Marie had been, she seemed to have less ability to stand up for herself. She was a year and a half younger but old enough to marry the father of her child. It was certainly a tough road for both sisters starting families so young. Marie somehow weathered the hardships, bouncing back at every setback. Melinda had a quieter personality never asking for anything. She had to grow up fast as she too married, following in her big sister's footsteps. Through time and healing, however, Thomas and Elizabeth began enjoying all their grandchildren, returning to some semblance of normalcy.

It was during this time period Thomas realized his daughters needed to have a career. With their parents' help, the girls went to cosmetology school. Just before Melinda graduated, she had developed severe allergies to chemicals and was unable to continue. Marie graduated, having won a first place award in a fantasy hairstyling contest. She made the newspaper, making her husband and father proud. She eventually opened her own salon in her home. Marie found this to be the best way to raise her daughter Lisa.

After nearly a decade of marriage, Marie and Larry divorced. Throughout their marriage, Larry often seemed troubled, disengaged, and appeared to suffer from depression. Due to the fact that it was a late teenage marriage and differences could not be overcome, they grew apart. A year after the divorce, Larry remarried and moved out of state. He and his second wife started a family, having two more children. Sadly he never looked back or reached out to his daughter Lisa after his move, in part due to his second wife's insecurities. From the beginning, Larry's wife discouraged any relationship between Lisa and her father as well as between Lisa and her half sister and brother.

Having no contact, Marie found it odd to get one last call from Larry 12 years later. It was almost midnight and the first thing Marie noticed was how different he sounded. Larry told her he was moving away and was sorry for not keeping in touch with their daughter. He also told Marie to make sure Lisa knew he loved her. Marie kept the conversation upbeat, telling him that his daughter would love a direct call or a surprise visit from him. Marie continued to have a gut feeling something was wrong.

The next morning, Larry's second wife called Marie to say she was divorcing him and taking their children. She told Marie she had bad news for her daughter Lisa and thought she needed to hear it from her mother. She said, "Larry had shot himself shortly after midnight." Marie was devastated because it happened right after they had spoken. With great sadness and mixed feelings, Marie realized she did the best she could and there was nothing she could have done to change the outcome. Sadly it had been another tragic event leaving a negative impact mainly on Marie's daughter Lisa.

Marie eventually found happiness the second time around. Her second marriage gave her daughter Lisa a wonderful stepfather. Lisa eventually married, giving Marie and Bob two beautiful grandchildren. They remained very close and involved, feeling fortunate to have watched their grandkids grow to become wonderful adults. Bob's been a blessing in Marie's life.

Going back again to the mid-'70s, during the time of Marie and Larry's marriage, Melinda's marriage was also falling apart. Her new husband Sam had become an alcoholic. He worked every day but would come home drunk much of the time. All she wanted was a loving husband and father to make a nice home for their little girl, Eva, with another child on the way. Melinda was a wonderful mother with little support. Her husband had been too young and immature to handle married life. Melinda tried desperately to hang on to her vows but there were too many obstacles in the marriage. She loved her two little girls, wanting only the best for them. Due to the lack of support and trust, they divorced.

Unfortunately Melinda found new friends who negatively impacted her life. The one man she began to believe in gave false promises and Melinda could not see him for who he was. She married for a second time. Soon after, he became abusive and she realized she now had to entrust her children with her sister-in-law. She prayed to find her way back to her beautiful little girls whom she loved so dearly. As hard as she tried, Melinda's self-worth was deteriorating rapidly. She became depressed with feelings of hopelessness causing a downward spiral.

Another Tragedy Soon Takes Place

Unfortunately, one never knows another's breaking point and it's almost impossible to know how badly someone is hurting. Everyone wants to feel secure and loved, but for Melinda, her grip on life was loosening. Marie began to see the severity of her depression and with help from Sara, the youngest sister, they brought Melinda to a hospital for an evaluation. Marie told the doctor that she needed close supervised care because Melinda had mentioned suicide. Marie was very unhappy with this doctor. He said, 'Melinda was just looking for attention.' His answer was to give her a strong drug for the treatment of depression. Marie didn't feel comfortable with this evaluation but, with little control and frustration, Melinda released herself after 24 hours. Marie still saw the same signs and with gut intuition she felt Melinda wasn't coming out of that dark place. Marie felt her sister had lost all hope of getting her beautiful little girls back. Melinda went back to her abuser in hopes he would change so that she could raise her little girls. The family did everything they could but no one could fill the void Melinda herself could not fill. Her life became an uphill battle. Marie believes the loss of her sweet baby girls in her life and the deep depression became far too painful to bear.

With great sadness and disbelief, the families worst fear had come true: Melinda overdosed with the very medication the doctor had prescribed. She was in a deep coma for three weeks before her passing. It nearly destroyed her parents, which had a rippling affect throughout the family. Unfortunately for any sibling who faces this kind of loss, they too become affected, not only by the loss of their sibling, but by their parent's grief, mostly due to parents being all consumed with guilt and loss. There is an expectation to be strong, which can become a huge burden by itself. When feelings become repressed, siblings may respond by pushing down the pain. Long-term effects often come out of feelings not being addressed. At the very least, bouts of sadness are often experienced throughout life. Families of suicide also become acutely aware of the stigmatism often associated with this act. Unfortunately, this kind of loss gives siblings reason to enter into the bargain of silence. Somehow, it takes on a form of protection. Suicide is not only difficult to say, but much harder to grieve through.

This deep wrenching heartache continued taking its toll on both Thomas and Elizabeth. To compound the pain, 24 years later their sweet granddaughter Eva, Melinda's oldest daughter, was struggling with depression as well. Her life also was lost to this horrible brain disease. Sadly, Eva passed away at the very same age as her mother. Both were only '24 years' young, two beautiful women gone before their time.

As the sun broke through the darkest of clouds, the healing process began yet again. The remaining Herndon children went on with their busy lives, burying the pain as best they could. For a parent, suicide can cause deep heartache and despair, sometimes breaking the strongest. Yet over time, it was the strength and support within the family that brought both parents and their remaining children through another difficult time.

When time allowed for healing, Thomas Sr. would often sit and tell stories of happier times. These memories shared with his family brought him great comfort. He often spoke of the positive impact his grandmother had on his life. She was a beautiful

Micmac Indian from Nova Scotia named Nora, who passed away at 93. Thomas Sr. so admired her strength and spirit. He loved the ancient sayings and stories she often shared. It was these great words of wisdom that helped shape his life. The most memorable moment in time was when he sat by her bedside holding her hand as she lay dying. She told him not to be afraid. Nora spoke of her spiritual beliefs. She said to her grandson that there would be no spiritual death as she would pass from one world to the next. She said that one day they would all be together in that same place of light.

The Herndons Continue on Life's Journey

Thomas and Elizabeth's youngest daughter Sara had the most outgoing personality. The combination of a larger-than-life personality and Sara's humorous ability to avoid conflict was one of her best qualities. Sara could find her way out of anything and, if she were to find trouble, she always knew what to do. A situation recalled by her oldest sister was a time when Sara was in elementary school. One day, walking home from school with friends, they all came upon that once familiar red box called a fire alarm. Being the jokester she was, Sara thought it would be fun to pull the alarm and run. When the fire and police arrived at the Herndon residence, they asked Sara if she had anything to do with pulling the alarm. Her answer was simply, 'No, her older brother Thomas did it.' Of course this was not the case, but at that point the fire (that never occurred) was extinguished. Thomas Jr. had a great alibi: he wasn't home. Certainly, things calmed down and Sara didn't have to face a direct hit. I believe this was the beginning of showing her father she would stand up to anything, and, if she couldn't, she knew to keep the escape hatch open. Sara had another loving family in the neighborhood that was her 'go to' as a young teen. This young Italian family was a much needed balance for her.

There is an advantage of being a middle child: one in particular is avoiding mistakes made by older siblings. Sara soon learned she was not going to walk the same path as her two older sisters. She would have that big wedding and children wouldn't figure into it, at least not for some time. Sara fell in love with an older doctor, married, and enjoyed the good times. They traveled, enjoying the finer things in life. However, after some years of marriage, she noticed his drinking became too much and the age difference was not making for a compatible situation. She eventually divorced and found her true soul mate, and they went on to have two beautiful children.

One often hears from parents that, in some respects, raising boys seems easier than girls. Surely that can be argued. However, for Thomas and Elizabeth, their three boys seemed to be the least problematic to them. There was a 10- and 11-year difference in ages between Thomas Jr. and his two younger brothers. James, the youngest, was the last to leave home. While growing up, the boys avoided any serious trouble. Maybe their dad being a cop played a role in their behavior. They got into things as all boys do, but nothing that warranted heavy discipline. Being close in age, the two youngest seemed to get along quite well. Matthew, being a year older than James and more expressive, seemed to get more of his parents' attention. He also found ways to get things he wanted, sometimes without much effort. Matthew knew how to get out of the way of trouble at home. He would shut his door and play his guitar, sometimes shutting out the world. Matthew was a talented musician with a voice much like Neil Young. His sisters loved to hear him sing 'Old Man' and 'Stairway to Heaven.' Matthew's dad once sat with him, singing along and listening to his version of 'Help' by the Beetles. That particular song seemed to emanate those sad feelings Thomas Sr. often struggled with.

Another story shared by his sister was about a prank Matthew pulled on his brother James. As a young teen, Matthew wanted to build a room in the basement—the kind of room you would need for music, strobe lights, built in speakers, and a door to keep the music from traveling. The problem he found was there was no heat coming into the space, and so he made his own. He discovered a great solution: by rearranging some of the metal heating ducts, of course not knowing the heat was being taken from James's room. Matthew was ingenious for his age, it worked beautifully! Of course James did find himself adding more blankets every winter and not knowing why. The good news is that it became one of those childhood prank stories they both now share with laughter.

Just the same, boys will be boys. All experiences become a part of life's journey. Matthew turned out to be a very talented young man who went on to become jack-of –all-trades! He went from building a room in the basement to turning his first van into a camper with built-ins. Matthew even made his own guitars! Once married, Matthew built his first beautiful home and had three wonderful children. He then started and maintained a successful business, making his dad and children proud!

James' personality was much like his late sister Melinda's. He was on the quiet side and not as outgoing as his older siblings. He often helped his mother and father out, being the last to leave home. James was the son who gave the least resistance by doing what was asked of him. Making excuses for why he couldn't did not come natural for James. His oldest brother Thomas was off on his own and James worked hard at filling his big brother's shoes. He was a great help to his dad throughout much of his life. James moved from his parent's home in his early thirties.

It was around this same time period in 1987 that Elizabeth had sadly and unexpectedly passed away. She did not survive the much-needed heart bypass surgery even though the family had plans for her return home. Never waking from surgery, Elizabeth died unexpectedly at the age of 70. This loss left Thomas devastated and depressed. With help from his siblings, James made a separate apartment in his home to help his dad in his later years. Thomas Sr. was not used to living alone as it made him anxious and depressed. Elizabeth had been the glue that kept the family together. Her death brought feelings of great sadness and loss as family members found ways to cope as best they could.

Years had passed when James announced he was getting married. He had just become a Certified Financial Planner. However, he continued in law enforcement like his older brother and dad before him. After paying off his house, James married Maura, giving both him and his new wife the ability to help his father in his senior years. Thomas had remained physically fit and active well into his 80's. There was no need for caregiving until he found a much needed companion just a few years older. She was a lovely lady named Beth, who married him. Although Beth was very active when they met, it wasn't long into the marriage when she broke her hip and needed care. James and his wife, along with Sara who lived nearby, played a major role in the care of Beth before her passing.

Thomas Sr. had James help both him and Beth with their finances. Problems came within the family when their finances weren't being discussed. Much of this happened during a time period when the markets crashed and many lost their savings all across the country. This created a time of family separation due to siblings upset over the loss of money. Monetary affairs can split the best of families and it's far too common. The good news is that in time, the Herndon siblings realized having family connection was far more valuable than money. The loss of so many family members may have played an important role in mending fences. After all, life can be gone in a blink of an eye leaving no chance for forgiveness or goodbyes. The Herndon siblings deeply understood that.

James and his wife Maura went on to have two beautiful boys. Their marriage started out with much love and devotion, however, over the years it had become strained. James' past losses had caught up, forcing him to take a hard look at why he felt angry much of the time. What was it that caused all this misdirected anger? In time he began to realize the loss of so many family members, including his twin, which had never truly been addressed. Over the years feelings of sadness and grief had been pushed down. Due to his line of work as a police officer, he saw so much injustice and needless deaths. James wore the same uniform as his oldest brother and dad, all three serving the public. A few years back he had been the first officer to arrive at a relative's home after he had shot himself. This kind of trauma over the years can become deeply embedded, such as in the cases of the many vets with PTSD. Once he became acutely aware, and with God's help, the healing process slowly began. Over time, James had become a patient and loving father to his two boys enjoying every moment with them.

Elizabeth Herndon – Death Certificate: 'Broken Heart Syndrome'

Four years before Elizabeth's death in 1987, the most shocking tragedy occurred. It was the final blow. Her death certificate read she had died from 'Broken Heart Syndrome.' This is now a documented tragic syndrome within the medical community. The horrific death of her oldest son was the final blow that did irreparable damage to her heart and soul. These unexpected tragedies deeply affected all of the Herndon family.

Back in the late '70s and early '80s, the oldest sibling Thomas Jr. had been married to his beautiful wife and they had three children and were living the American dream. He had graduated from the State Police Academy, working lots of overtime through the years. Thomas Jr. was a hard worker, loved his family, and like a kid, enjoyed fun times. He loved family parties, cookouts, and gatherings. He enjoyed all the neighborhood kids, bringing them together to play baseball. In his yard, Thomas Jr. built an official-looking 'Green Monster' wall similar to the one at Fenway Park. All the neighborhood kids got to play ball no matter what age or how well they played—they all loved and looked up to Thomas!

Thomas Jr. was a loving son, brother, husband, and father. Thomas Sr. once shared a heartfelt story about the two oldest when they were small children. Marie's big brother Thomas was 5 at the time and Marie just 2. Thomas Jr. would often take his little sister's hand, walking her over to see the goats on the family farm. One day Thomas Jr. noticed one of the goats was trying to eat his little sister's curls. He went in for the save, turning Marie's tears into laughter. The story of how Thomas Jr. made the save was only known among the three! This story of how he protected his little sister made them both beam with pride!

Marie now sees her life as coming full circle. She moved back to the hill in her twenties, living out the remainder of her life. Generations of the Herndon family, including her great-grandmother Nora, the

Micmac Indian, had all lived on the many acres of farmland. Although there is no longer farming and much of the land has been sold off, it's now a quiet cul-de-sac. Marie continues to feel a deep spiritual connection there, especially to her great-grandmother, though she died before Marie was born.

Going back to the early '70s, shortly after Thomas Jr. had graduated from the State Police Academy, he began working the night shift. It was during this time he lost his sister Melinda. Thomas Jr. would leave work at 11:00 pm, driving several miles to spend those last days with her. The night nurse told a family member that Thomas Jr. often talked to Melinda, holding her hand as she lay in a deep coma. No matter what the weather, he never missed a night. Everyone had admired his family devotion.

After Thomas's marriage, busy schedule or not, he looked forward to his weekly visits with his mother. Elizabeth had loved making her famous apple pies when she knew Thomas would be stopping by. He loved her pies topped with vanilla ice cream. Thomas also loved watching sports with his dad, often having him to his house to watch the Bruins games. The best of the best played in the late '60s and '70s. There was Wayne Gretzky, Phil Esposito, and Bobby Orr, to name a few. And oh, how great those Bruins were back then!

Oftentimes, Thomas Jr. would tell funny stories of different incidents at work. One in particular was during a traffic stop. Back in the '70s, he approached a driver who had big red hair, similar to Ronald McDonald. When Thomas asked for his license and registration, he took it back to his cruiser and to his disbelief, discovered the man had the same name: Ronald McDonald!!! Thomas had to call it in to make sure there were no outstanding warrants. He hesitated because, just as expected, as soon as he called in the name the police radio went silent. With no surprise to Thomas, jokes came pouring through the airwaves with laughter— *"Trooper Herndon, did you check the trunk for burgers?"* Thomas decided even though Ronald was going over the speed limit, having that name along with the bushy red hair was enough reason for letting him go!

There also was a particular story that was told to a family member but never shared by Thomas Jr. It's the silent heroism that our police officers and troopers never talk about. It's part of their job. They are the brave men and women in blue. However, this particular story is well worth sharing. There is much that goes on behind scenes that the public never hears: the heroic acts our officers do that rarely make news.

Thomas responded to a call on a busy highway. There was a car, off the road in a ditch that had been there for some time. He arrived to find an unconscious mother and a baby that wasn't breathing. Trooper Herndon picked up the baby and began mouth-to-mouth resuscitation. At the same time he called for an ambulance, leaving another trooper there with the mother. He knew it would take several minutes for the ambulance to arrive with heavy traffic. Thomas kept the child in his arms as he proceeded to a nearby hospital while giving life support. He felt it would have been the best chance at reviving the infant. After the baby was examined, the doctors reported that there would have been no way to save the baby boy due to the length of time the infant had stopped breathing. It left many sleepless nights for Thomas as he wished he had been at the scene much sooner. These difficult situations are hard on any officer or rescuer because when they arrive they never know what they will see or find.

The Herndons' Most Tragic Event (1983)

One cold February night, Thomas Jr. was off for the evening, enjoying his wife and three children. He received a call from work that a trooper called in sick and the unit was shorthanded. They needed him to do a double shift. Of course he was devoted to his work and his family understood that. After all, he was the breadwinner. Thomas jumped back in his cruiser, officially back on duty.

That evening Megan, his wife, received a phone call from a relative saying that he had heard on his scanner a trooper was shot but had no details. He was hoping Thomas' wife would say he was home. No sooner had Megan hung up when she dialed the barracks where her husband was stationed. Her stomach sank and she dropped the phone. Within minutes the State Police were at her door. In the meantime, Thomas' parents were also notified and the State Police picked up his parents along with Marie. According to Marie, it was the longest, most painful ride she had ever experienced. The hospital that Thomas was taken to was over 25 miles away. Thomas Sr. sat silent in the front seat of the cruiser while Marie tried to help her mother in the back as she was having difficulty catching her breath.

As they entered the hospital, there was a deafening silence everywhere. Several officials came forward, accompanying the family to the elevator. Marie tried signaling to one of them to find out if her brother had made it. The gentlemen put his head down. It was at that moment she knew she had lost her brother. Her next thought was to stay strong for her parents. She took a deep breath, pushing down the most painful feelings. From then on it all became a blur. Reality was setting in, the incident unfolded, and tears flowed. While facts began to sink in, the most painful heartache began for the Herndon family.

Trooper Thomas Herndon had conducted a motor vehicle stop not far from the main highway. In a secluded area, he stopped a small car due to a rear light out and when approaching the vehicle noticed three men inside. Unbeknownst to Thomas, these men had guns and were plotting an armed robbery. Thomas asked them to get out of the car and all three started to converse to each other in Spanish. Without warning, Trooper Herndon was shot in the leg during a struggle. After being shot three more times he tried to crawl back to his cruiser. One of the men proceeded to jump on him, pumping three more bullets into his back. The perpetrators also shot out his tire, confiscated his wallet and his gun, tore off his wedding ring, and jumped into their vehicle to escape. After being shot seven times, Thomas, with all the strength he had, stood up in the middle of the road to flag a vehicle down. One gentleman got out of a pickup to assist by calling an ambulance, and another followed the suspected vehicle hoping to identify the perpetrators. A brave man he turned out to be. It was this gentleman's testimony that identified these three murderers, getting them life sentences with no parole. This family endured three separate and highly publicized trials over a period of two years.

Sadly, his family did not make it in time to be by Thomas's side to say goodbye. Somehow he held on to life for 1½ hours waiting to speak with a priest before he took his last breath. Thomas Jr. held his religion close to his vest. * *In his cruiser over his visor there was a beautiful prayer which is shared at the end of this chapter.*

Each one of the Herndons handled this horrific tragedy as best they could. The siblings believed it was that night that played a big part in their mother's death. The glint of happiness had disappeared from her eyes, as hard as she tried. Family members often caught her crying as she went through the motions of life. Elizabeth's tears never completely stopped. Due to years of tears within and that fateful last blow, doctors were unable to repair Elizabeth's broken heart.

In the meantime, Thomas Sr. needed answers. He did not know how to rid this horrific pain deep inside. With a passion fueled by loss and anger, he began his most difficult journey. He wanted to be sure these savage murderers could never walk free. He also wanted to see the death penalty reinstated for first degree murder with brutal atrocity. At 70 years old, Thomas began his campaign in favor of the death penalty to protect our first line of defense, our men and women in blue. He worked tirelessly for over 10 years, but Massachusetts, being one of the most liberal states in the country, had banned the death penalty. Thomas Sr. had many supporters, backers, and friends, including the former and late Governor King, Governor Weld, Governor Mitt Romney, the late

Paul Cellucci, Andy Card, and other elected officials. Due to the newly elected liberal Governor Michael Dukakis, it had become a losing battle. Thomas Sr. would not give up. He began working with a woman whose brother was brutally beaten, thrown in a trash can, set on fire, and burned to death. The vicious murderer, Willie Horton, was a prisoner out on furlough. It was this horrific story that motivated both Thomas Sr. and the victim's sister to make changes in the law. The two worked tirelessly, getting well over 10,000 hand-written signatures to the governor's office to end the prison furlough program. During Dukakis' first term, he had vetoed a similar bill that would have stopped furloughs for first degree murderers. The result was the release of convicted murderer Willie Horton, who had gotten out on a furlough during Dukakis' second term and committed a brutal assault and rape. During Dukakis' run for the presidency, the Bush campaign used a very effective commercial entitled "Weekend Passes," showing a revolving prison door with prisoners coming and going. This highly publicized case became a primary factor in Governor Dukakis losing the presidential election. Representative Joseph Connolly, Thomas's friend and a former police officer, proposed a bill to stop these furloughs. This bill finally became law in Massachusetts, stopping first degree murderers from being allowed out on furloughs. Thomas' dedication and hard work had finally given him some peace of mind. In his mid-eighties he was honored in the State House for the passage of this bill. Surely murders have been prevented due to the enactment of the law which was signed in 1988.

There are many families who have gone through several losses over a lifetime. For some, one tragic loss is enough to change a piece of who they once were. Losses become tragic when nature has gone into reverse. Marie's father once said that parents represent the past, a spouse represents the present, and children represent the past, present, and future. A parent's future is never the same when a child is gone. The depth of desperation a parent feels is unimaginable. The Herndon family endured this pain and loss four different times, profoundly touching their lives.

With heavy hearts, the Herndon siblings remain positive and strong in spite of the emotional scars. Marie has shared her family's story to help others looking to stay on track, awaiting the light at the end of the tunnel. The light is promised with time. Her belief in prayer and support helped Marie and her family in surviving life's tragic circumstances.

The Prayer Found in the Cruiser
of Trooper Thomas Herndon

I have no idea where I am going. I do not see the road ahead of me. I cannot know for certain where it will end. Nor do I really know myself, and the fact that I think that I am following your will does not mean that I am actually doing so. But I believe this. I believe that the desire to please you does in fact please you. I hope I have that desire in everything I do. I hope I never do anything apart from that desire. And I know that if I do this you will lead me by the right road though I may know nothing about it at the time. Therefore I will trust you always for though I may seem to be lost, and in the shadow of death. I will not be afraid because I know you will never leave me, to face my troubles alone.

— from 'Thoughts in Solitude' by Thomas Merton

ST. CHRISTOPHER PROTECT US

~~~~~~~~~~~~~

In Trooper Herndon's Honor and for his Bravery,
The Commonwealth of Massachusetts under
Governor Michael Dukakis
Created the Trooper Thomas Herndon Medal of
Honor Award Ceremony

The Herndon Awards, which have been held annually since 1983, have become a symbol of prestige, within both the law enforcement community and the Commonwealth as a whole. This Award continues to be an opportunity to publicly recognize the bravery of members of the law enforcement community. These are the men and women who put their lives on the line each day by dedicating themselves to public safety throughout Massachusetts.

A Family Broken - Surviving Traumatic Loss

Chapter 3

Coping with Traumatic Loss of a Loved One

This book was written in memory of Thomas and Elizabeth Herndon

Joan, Melinda, Eva and Thomas Herndon Jr.

'Gone..,but never forgotten.'

There is nothing in life as painful as the traumatic death of a loved one. This kind of pain can never be described, only felt through experience. Facing these horrific emotions head on is the best and only option. Each and every person handles death in different ways and there is no right or wrong way. Some of us seem to move away from grief rather quickly, while others tend to hang on. There is no timeline.

Expressing yourself is important in dealing with this type of pain. Reaching out, letting tears flow, and talking about it often helps the healing process.

Many experts recommend confiding in someone and finding a support system which helps to make the journey less painful. One of the most important steps in facing loss head on is allowing time to become the healer. We can feel that no one understands, and very likely they don't. The best advice for well-meaning friends or family is just to be there, listen, and help with anything that is needed. Grief takes on a life of its own and those in mourning need to hang on to it until they are ready to let go. My hope is that this book will give strength to those feeling alone and in deep pain. We all CAN and DO find our way to the other side. Certainly the Herndons' story is a prime example.

This does not mean that some scars will not remain— they will. Time heals and we will notice good days becoming more frequent. Scars do fade and joyous moments will begin to return. We can let go without feeling guilty. We must not forget that loved ones who have passed before us would certainly want nothing more than for us to find happiness again.

As Marie became older, she found herself yearning more for those days of yesteryear, oftentimes with feelings of sadness. By sharing her story, she is now able to tap into the happier memories while letting go of the darker times. Keeping the wonderful memories of those she's loved and lost can only lead her to the light, bringing peace.

The strength that the Herndon family has shown has been astounding. We all know bad things happen, however, it's how we respond and deal with each tragedy that defines how we survive. One can choose to stay in perpetual sadness immobilized by the gravity of the loss or rise from the pain. Bereavement affects people differently, especially after a traumatic and unexpected death. However, those who have felt the deep sorrow and unrelenting pain of their darkest moments and survived become stronger. Personally I've never met a strong person who had an easy past.

Relationships are important, but any traumatic loss can change the dynamics. If the loss is within the family, there is generally a coming together. Family members often experience loss in different ways that can create difficulty in understanding one another. Trauma is a crisis and it can bring people together, but it can create strain and tension.

One of the most enlightening messages for Marie was from philosopher Eckhart Tolle. He basically stated that it's not the *things* that happen to you that your pain arises from, but your *reaction* to it. He also says: "Whenever something negative happens to you, there is a deep lesson concealed within it."

Most all of Marie's family tragedies seemed to be more in line with the tragedies of the Kennedy family—deep lessons not easily found!

Joseph P. Kennedy once wrote:

When the young bury the old, time heals the pain and sorrow.   But when the process is reversed, the sorrow remains forever.

~~~

When we understand that life happens to us all and we share with those who've walked in similar shoes, we can then begin to find a sense of peace.

Marie once said: "When tragedies happen and you make it to the other side, no mountain could be harder to climb."

Helpful Ideas in Coping with Traumatic Loss of a Loved One

Traumatic loss and grief can affect so much of who we are.

In the final chapter, coping skills and ideas are shared to help ease the pain of loss.

Feelings and reactions

Feelings and reactions can be strong with any trauma. There is no right or 'normal' response. One may experience these emotions in the hours, days, weeks, and months after a traumatic event. Feeling numb and in denial is not unusual. Feelings can also be very strong and frightening. One can feel loss of control, however crying is not an out-of-control reaction—it's perfectly normal. Even when you may feel you are 'going mad' or develop what seems like irrational fears, this too can be normal. However, if it goes on for too long or you feel the inability to cope with daily life, a support organization may be needed.

Common feelings for traumatic loss are sadness, longing, guilt, shame, anger, numbness, emptiness, or hopelessness about the future. These are all normal feelings when trying to cope with trauma.

1) Most experts agree that having the support of loved ones and talking with someone such as a friend, clergy, or someone who has experienced similar loss is so very important.

2) There is no timeline for grief. Take all the time you need!

3) Keeping a journal or writing down thoughts or feelings can be very helpful.

4) Take care and be kind to yourself, go on with life when YOU are ready!

5) Sometimes it is helpful to create new ideas for the holidays. For some, it can be difficult to continue old traditions.

Call your doctor if you

1) Experience intense yearning for the deceased not diminishing over time,

2) Become depressed for too long,

3) Feel unable to care for yourself,

4) Feel the need to start using or increasing the use of alcohol or drugs,

5) Feel unrealized anger that doesn't go away,

6) Have any thoughts of suicide.

Comments to avoid when comforting the bereaved

1) **"It's part of God's plan."**

This phrase can make people angry and they often respond with "What plan? Nobody told me about a plan."

2) **"Look at what you have to be thankful for."**

They know they have things to be thankful for, but right now those things are not important.

3) **"He or she is in a better place right now."**

The bereaved may or may not believe this. Keep your beliefs to yourself unless asked.

4) **"This is behind you now; it's time to get on with your life."**

Sometimes the bereaved are resistant to getting on with life because they feel this means "forgetting" their loved one. Besides, moving on is much easier said than done. Grief has a mind of its own and works at its own pace.

5) **Statements that begin with "You should..." or "You will..."**

These statements are too directive. Instead you could begin your comments with: "Have you thought about..." or "you might try..."

Source: American Hospice Foundation

"Everyone must leave something behind when he or she dies, my grandfather said. A child or a book or a painting or a house or a wall built or a pair of shoes made. Or a garden planted. Something your hand touched some way so your soul has somewhere to go when you die, and when people look at that tree or that flower you planted, you're there."

Ray Bradbury
Farenheit 451

Some of my research - written self-help and coping - Chapter 3 from : Duke University Health System Bereavement.

Cover art and design on pages 1, 5, 23, 57 by Brooke M. Delmonaco

Page 1 photo: Herndon family home, 1950s–1980s

Made in the USA
Middletown, DE
12 September 2020